The Sumerian Controversy
A SPECIAL REPORT

The Sumerian Controversy

A SPECIAL REPORT

*The Elite Power Structure Behind
the Latest Discovery Near Ur*

DR. HEATHER LYNN

The
MIDNIGHT CRESCENT
PUBLISHING CO.
TRADEMARK

Published by The Midnight Crescent Publishing Company,
Cleveland, Ohio, U.S.A.

Cover art by Chris DiAlfredi

ISBN-10: 1484836855
ISBN-13: 978-1484836859

Profits from the sale of this publication go to help fund the Society for Truth in Archaeological Research—STAR. Thank you for supporting truth. STAR is a member supported international organization of independent researchers and professionals interested in archaeology from a more inclusive perspective. Our aim is to help empower independent researchers through support, community, resources, and education, so that the truth about human history can be uncovered and shared.

To learn more about STAR, please visit www.societyfortruthinarchaeologicalresearch.org.

Printed and bound in the United States of America.

Contents

ix *Preface*

1 ONE · Origination

5 TWO · Discovery

15 THREE · Digging Deeper

23 FOUR · Evidence

35 FIVE · Moving Forward

43 SIX · More Information

A Note from Heather...

Every day, amazing discoveries are being made in the field of science. Through the barrage of messages and white noise of commercialism, many have begun to wake up to the control mechanisms and propaganda of the mainstream.

I think we truly are experiencing a paradigm shift. People all over are increasingly interested in learning alternative perspectives. This is evident in the success of shows like *Ancient Aliens*, *America Unearthed*, *Coast to Coast AM*, and many more. Alternative media is on the rise and is becoming less of a subcultural product and more of a world awakening. The people have banded together through the power of the internet. We have positioned ourselves as a major player in the world of mass communication as a diverse community of many interests, philosophies, and ideologies. Each individual has a special skill or talent to bring to the roundtable of truth. Together we can stand united against those who are determined to suppress this truth.

This is why I've started an organization called the Society for Truth in Archaeological Research (STAR). It is a member supported international organization of independent researchers and professionals interested in archaeology from a more inclusive perspective. The goal is to help empower people through support, community, resources, and education to uncover the truth about human history. Then, present it to the public so that they can make up their own minds. The profits from this publication go to support STAR so that we may build a community of truth-seekers, unified in solving the mysteries of humanity's origins.

As George Orwell said, "Who controls the past controls the future. Who controls the present controls the past." I believe that if enough people join together to uncover the truth about our past, we can take back control of our future.

Thank you again, for supporting STAR.

Preface

The following special report is the beginning part of a series called, *Mysteries in Mesopotamia*. I have decided that rather than wait to publish my research, it is important that I release the information as I receive it. This explains if there may appear to be gaps or inconclusive evidence. My investigation is a work in progress. The goal of publishing my preliminary findings is to ensure that my research is open, transparent, and inclusive. One thing is certain; what I have published in this initial report is only the tip of the iceberg. Much of the evidence I have seen points to something missing, perhaps the real reason we have invaded this region, the real reason this research has been undertaken, or what is really buried in the desert. Could there be lost technology, as some have claimed? Could there be evidence supporting scripture or ancient texts? Could there be some clue as to the true origin of humanity?

These questions and more are looming as I go in search of what is really behind the latest discovery near Ur and expose the 'Mysteries in Mesopotamia'. Come with me down the rabbit hole.

ONE

Origination

. . . . . .

My journey started when I opened my Facebook messages on a chilly morning in March, 2013. As someone who appears regularly on paranormal and alternative radio talk shows, I tend to get a lot of emails containing research leads or requests to look into various phenomena. This is why it did not come as a surprise to see an email from a gentleman claiming to have knowledge of a new discovery near the ancient Mesopotamian city of Ur.

Though intrigued, I was fairly skeptical because there have not been excavations in the region (that we know of) for many years. The political climate in modern day Iraq has made research a dangerous and unwelcome task. Knowing this, I opened and started reading the email with a type of curious skepticism that I so often have when approaching these topics.

You see, I am a skeptic. Not in a Michael Shermer type way, however. I prefer to think of it as more of a Dana Scully type skepticism that has its roots in the fact that I come from a scientific background. I am open to new ideas and I believe that there is a place for creativity in science. Historical figures like Sir Isaac Newton have demonstrated that hard science can benefit from open-minded inquiry. That being said, I eagerly but cautiously, read the message to see what sort of lead this gentleman thought he had. The message read:

> "Dear Dr. Heather Lynn,
> Please help. I have knowledge of artefacts that have been found at a site called Tel Khyber in Iraq they are taking bags and bags away. THIS IS OUR HERITAGE! Please help! What can we do? Profits from the dust of our people are disgrace...Blessings to you, Abdulsamad"

As I read the message, I felt powerless. If this were true, how could I help? What could I do? I am sitting in my home office in my pajamas with a cup of coffee reading this desperate plea. I am a writer and researcher, not a superhero. Still, I felt a sense of responsibility to take action. First, I would have to investigate a bit further to verify what little information I had.

Starting with the source, I clicked on Abdulsamad's profile photo only to find that his profile was set to private. I could not tell much about who he was from his profile so I messaged him back, asking if he had any more details and assuring him that I would do whatever I could to look into this matter and help in any way possible.

As the day progressed, I never heard back from him. I had a full schedule ahead of me so I could not actively pursue the matter. I decided to revisit it in the evening, if time would allow.

That night, I closed myself into my office, turned on some of the peaceful sounds of Bach's Orchestral Suite No. 3 in D major, and started burning the midnight oil. I researched mainstream sources and exclusive academic databases to no avail. Certainly there would be something online about this if it were true. Perhaps there was a translation or spelling issue, since Abdulsamad's message appeared to have a pattern of broken English. After trying various methods of searching, I feared this may not be a viable lead. Still, I felt drawn to the story because if it were true, the implications were enormous. We may be on the cusp of new revelations about our past and the history of the Sumerian civilization.

A few days passed and I found no information on the new site, nor did I speak with Abdulsamad again. Then suddenly, my phone buzzed to alert me of a news release that had gone out from the *Christian Science Monitor*. Here it was; the new site, Tell Khaiber! My hunch was right. It must have been the spelling error that had prevented some of the progress during my preliminary internet searches. As my heart raced, my skepticism crumbled like the ruins of a once great city. Now, perhaps I could make some headway!

TWO

Discovery

. . . . . .

T HE DISCOVERY ITSELF IS SO SPECTACULAR, that even the mainstream had to take notice. A team of British archaeologists had discovered a previously unknown structure they believe to be a place of great historic significance near the ancient city of Ur. The name Ur is the same as the Hebrew verb ('or) meaning to be or to become light or to shine. Thus, Ur is the city of light. For those familiar with the spectacular Sumerian creation myths, this is quite a fitting name.

This was the first foreign excavation at the site in southern Iraq since the 1930s. Referring of course, to the last major excavation at Ur conducted by a British/American team led by Sir Charles Leonard Woolley, son of George Herbert Woolley, in the 1920s and the 1930s. After the 1950s revolution, which toppled Iraq's monarchy, a nearby military air base put the area off limits to foreign archaeologists for sixty years.

To give you a bit of a back story, Woolley is often considered to be one of the first "modern" archaeologists. This iconic-looking figure of the glory days of archaeology was even knighted in 1935 for his contributions to the field. He was also one of the first archaeologists to propose that the flood described in the Biblical Book of Genesis was a local event, after he had identified flood-stratum at Ur.

C. Leonard Woolley (left) and T. E. Lawrence at the archaeological excavations at Carchemish, Syria, circa 1912-1914.

Woolley began his archaeological career in 1906, later stating that he "had never studied archaeological methods even from books ", and "..had not any idea how to make a survey or a ground-plan..." (Woolley 1953). By today's standards he would be considered an amateur and not even permitted to research, let alone excavate, but Woolley found spectacular treasures that rivaled those of King Tutankhamen's tomb and continued to advance the field of archaeology by making great discoveries throughout the near east.

Amid the monuments Woolley and his team found at Ur were the bodies of royalty, adorned with elaborate gold jewelry, including a queen's headdress made of gold leaves and studded with lapis lazuli. Other objects included a gold and lapis lyre, one of the first known musical instruments, jewelry, cups, and other household furnishings. All of these treasures were subsequently split between the British Museum, the newly created Iraq Museum, and the University of Pennsylvania, which funded Woolley's work.

Woolley and his team had the rare opportunity to explore tombs with enormous paintings of ancient Sumerian culture at the height of its grandeur. Much of this art depicts winged beings and what some have described as giants. All around the figures is cuneiform writing, telling tales of lineage and birth-right. The most extravagant tomb found at the time was that of Queen Pu-Abi, which had been surprisingly undisturbed by looters. Also discovered were the now famous cylindrical seals bearing her name in Sumerian. They also found a number of figurines including one referred to as "Ram in a Thicket"—a beautiful, but odd looking piece.

Sumerian cylindrical seal.

Many experts theorize that a mere 10 percent of the artifacts in this region have been unearthed. Understandably, researchers have avoided Ur and the surrounding sites for safety concerns. With the exception of a few small groups, including

Continued on page 11

One of two
"Ram in a Thicket"
figures, discovered
at Ur by Woolley

Soldiers standing guard.

U.S. Army Brig. Gen. Michael Lally, left front, and Col. Dan Hokanson, behind Lally, lead Soldiers down steps of the Ziggurat of Ur during a tour outside Camp Adder, Iraq, July 31, 2009.

the Global Heritage Fund (GHF), an NGO based in California, people have mostly stayed away. The site is currently on UNESCO's tentative list of world heritage sites.

It is amazing that the site has been so neglected. As it is referred to in the Bible, Ur of the Chaldeans was one of the greatest urban centers of the Sumerian civilization until its conquest by Alexander the Great a few centuries before Jesus. It is believed to have peaked between 2112 and 2095 BCE, under the rule of King Ur-Nammu. With all of these treasures and rich cultural resources having been discovered, what happened? Why have archaeologists stayed away? The Ziggurat was partially restored in the 1960s, but otherwise, the entire site has been described as undergoing "a slow process of erosion" due to neglect, according to Italian art historian, Alessandro Bianchi, who has spent time training six Iraqis in special restoration techniques in an effort to save Ur.

The site is frequently subjected to strong wind, extreme heat, and excessive salinity of the soil. In addition to the rough climate, the site has been frequently damaged due to the presence of Iraqi military bases that were bombed during the Gulf War. At one point, the establishment of the US military's Contingency Operating Base Adder, actually helped save Ur from the looting and violence, common to Iraq's archaeological sites. Still, these were military men, not archaeologists or preservationists. All they could do was guard the site. Were they really guarding the site, or something else?

Between wars and violence over the past 30 years, Ur was officially closed to foreign archaeologists. In 2003, the US invaded the area to remove Saddam Hussein from power. This left Baghdad's struggling government and economy to deal with greater priorities than funding large-scale archaeological excavations. They are rightfully more concerned about rebuilding their current cities than rebuilding cities from the past. Still, this is a tragic scenario.

Naturally, when recent satellite images showed the presence of large buildings presumed to be at least four thousand years old in the region near Ur, researchers saw this as an amazing opportunity. This new site, Tell Khaiber, is massive. Located more than 10 miles from Ur, it is the first major archaeological find that far from the city center. The actual excavation of the site officially broke ground in March, 2013 as a joint collaboration between British and Iraqi teams. This six-member British team worked with four Iraqis to dig in the southern province of Thi Qar, some 200 miles south of Baghdad.

A photograph of Ur from the air.
(*History and Monuments of Ur*, by C. J. Gadd)

Three weeks of work at Tell Khaiber confirmed the presence of at least one monumental building. Satellite images showed it to be square, and to measure at least 250 square feet. The rooms excavated along the eastern side of the building have solid pavements of regular mud bricks. One large hall, has a series of beautifully decorated floors leading the researchers to believe that the building was indeed, very important, if not sacred.

Another clue that this sprawling complex was important is the fact that the walls are nine feet thick. It is a monumental complex with rows of rooms encircling a grand courtyard. It is extremely unusual to find complexes this old at this scale. Using modern archaeological methods, researchers are also trying to test soil samples to determine information about climate, agriculture, and possible additional uses for this building. Early theories have been that it is a temple, palace, or possibly an "administrative center", dating back at least 4,000 years. If it is an administrative center, the possibility of a hall of records cannot be ruled out. Depending on what they find, this could be the most important discovery of our generation.

Some of the artifacts reported to be found at first were a 3 ½ inch clay plaque, depicting a worshiper dressed in a long fringed robe and some assorted pottery fragments. Excited about the prospect of what more may be found, I was eager to post this story to my archaeology loving friends on Facebook and my blog followers. So I did just that on March 28, 2013. Little did I realize I had only scratched the surface of a secret buried deep beneath the sand.

THREE

Digging Deeper

. . . . . .

IN THE DAYS TO FOLLOW, I TRIED TO LOCATE Abdulsamad to explain to him that I was aware of the situation but still wanted his thoughts on the issue. It is one thing to pass along a news story, but it is another to plea for someone's help. My gut was telling me that there was more to this story than what the mainstream media was putting out for public consumption. So naturally, I had to dig deeper.

Unfortunately, Abdulsamad's Facebook profile had been deleted. Now, I was really perplexed. Also a little strange and unsettling, was that upon opening my email I found that I had death threats! What on Earth would possess someone to send death threats for simply publishing a story about archaeology; especially when the story was pretty basic and came from a mainstream press release? This was getting stranger by the minute.

As I went to post to my blog, I noticed harassing comments were waiting in my comment moderation box too. I couldn't believe it. Were these really directed towards me? These comments included profanity, name calling, death threats, and accusations of my story being, of all things, a hoax! I wondered how this could be when clearly I did not make up the story of the newest discovery near Ur. The story came from a legitimate press release and by this point had already been published on a variety of mainstream media outlets including *Live Science, Fox News, The Daily Beast*, and a myriad of local and regional sites. As skeptical as I am and being leery of mainstream news sources, I considered the possibility of the story being a hoax. These days, it seems more difficult to trust anyone, especially those we are told by mainstream media to look to as authority. This called for more research, as my reputation, and possibly my safety was now on the line.

My next step was to actually pin down the few universities involved. On their sites, I saw press releases and photos confirming the mainstream news stories about the Tell Khaiber site, so I felt quite reassured that this was no hoax. I would prefer to get behind something I have seen with my own two eyes, but since I could not feasibly go to Iraq, I decided to get involved with the head of the project in Britain at the University of Manchester.

Being an academic, myself, I had no qualms about contacting the Professor to inquire about the new discovery. I looked at is an opportunity to "talk shop", if you will. Everyone in the administration was polite and helpful. I was granted the opportunity to interview the Professor via email. I was thrilled at the prospect, but it looked like I may have had to postpone the meeting, as I was leaving town to attend the Ancient Mysteries International Spring Conference.

Regardless of how busy I was, I knew I had to get to the bottom of this discovery. After all, this is our collective history. We deserve to know what is going on. There was no time to waste. I decided that rather than to drive across the states to the conference, I would board a train and use that time to work. I took this opportunity to tell my Facebook friends and followers to contact me with any questions they would like answered by the Professor. I really wanted this to be a chance for people to participate in the discussion.

I expected to get requests to ask the professor about topics that critics would view as "fringe", topics such as the Annunaki, time travel, stargates, etc., so I thought for quite a while on how I would pose these questions without being turned away. Here is an excerpt from the email I sent:

Hello Professor C...,

Congratulations on your team's recent discovery near Ur and thank you for allowing me a few questions. Your team has been very kind. As I explained, I have an outreach organization in the U.S. that tries to promote public interest and truth in archaeology and anthropology. The unfortunate truth is that there is a lot of misinformation circulating about the Sumerian culture so I do appreciate your help in promoting truth in archaeological research.

Here are my questions:

1. It is encouraging to know that there is a multi-cultural effort taking place on this project. In your opinion, how promising is the future of archaeology and cultural resource management in Iraq?

2. So much mystery has surrounded the general area around the excavation site due to a lack of ability to excavate over the years. What do you make of various speculations and theories regarding the ancient Sumerians (aliens, time-travelers, various religious significance, etc.)?

3. The site has been referred to as a possible "administrative center". Would you care to elaborate about what activities may have occurred there?
4. Finally, have there been any inscriptions or texts found; anything that could be read and subsequently

interpreted to give a more holistic view of the Sumerian culture?

Thank you very much for your generosity today, Professor C... I do wish you great success in your research and many more breathtaking finds!

Best Regards,
Dr. Heather Lynn
(440) 941-7713
heather@drheatherlynn.com

As the train whistled through my journey, I felt that I had done the most that I could do at that point and all that was left was to wait. Awaiting a response, I went about my business, hoping to have an answer within the week. A week passed, and no response. I tried several times to get back in touch with the contacts that I initially had made at the university, but no one would respond. I did a little detective work by going through my web analytics only to discover that shortly after receiving my email; the professor did a little research of his own and found out who I was. He had visited my site and that was the end of that.

I will leave you to be the judge of how I presented my inquiry to the professor, but by my calculations, I do not believe I came across as unprofessional, demanding, unfriendly, or disrespectful. I simply wanted to find out a little more than what was offered in the previously published mainstream articles. I felt it important to be an advocate on behalf of the people who follow my posts, listen to my interviews, and reach out to me in the hopes of finding the truth. Apparently, these people do not matter in the eyes of the establishment. This type of elitist thinking is what gives academia, and subsequently, education in general a bad name. Anti-intellectualism flourishes in today's society as apparent by the love of reality television, junk food, and apathy. This has to stop. We have to reclaim knowledge and celebrate inquiry and creativity in a more inclusive way.

To his credit, I will say that not knowing all of the details behind his lack of communication with me, we cannot judge too harshly. I have worked with professors before. Many of my dearest friends have been or are tenured professors. I am all too familiar with the limitations they face at the hands of the establishment. In some cases, simply addressing these issues can cause tenure to be questioned. Before passing judgment, one should ask: "How easy would it be to lose my livelihood and all that I have worked for in the name of ideology?" I have compassion for those open-minded individuals who work within academia to push the envelope incrementally, but remain trapped under the politics of the establishment. I know it can be frustrating, if not outright depressing.

This is why I had to break out of the mainstream, before I got too deeply intertwined. I decided it was better to stand on the side of truth, even if that meant a severe loss of income and a sullied reputation. A reputation apparently so bad, that you cannot even have an email considered worthy of a response.

After being rejected by the academic establishment, I decided it was still worth investigating. Only this time, I charted a course that rarely comes up dry. I followed the money.

FOUR

Evidence

· · · · · ·

S O BACK TO MY OFFICE, ARMED ONCE AGAIN WITH Bach, coffee, and a search engine, I dug deeper into the funding behind the recent discovery in Tell Khaiber. Doing so led me to find the usual big corporate and government backing, so I wasn't completely surprised, just disappointed, when I started unraveling more of the picture.

Here is the breakdown thus far, in the most straightforward sense. The main corporate backer to this operation is big oil; Gulfsands Petroleum, to be specific. The archaeologists actually report to this company on what they find. Gulfsands Petroleum was once a Houston, Texas based oil company with American directors. They are even listed as one of the founders of the excavation project. In 2008 the US Treasury Department declared that Gulfsands Petroleum was benefitting from corruption and implementing power plays by using Syrian intelligence officials to intimidate certain Syrian cabinet ministers, enabling them to gain access to lucrative oil exploration. The US imposed sanctions on Gulfsands so the company fled the country and relocated their operation to London.

Gulfsands' board reads like a roster of global banking heads and corporate interest. They are frequently involved in corruption scandals and routinely dodge EU sanctions. In some cases they have been referred to as a "propaganda tool", having intertwined with global politics and rushing to become a member of the UN Global Compact in September, 2011.

Also notable, is the self-aggrandizing way in which this oil company promotes its involvement in the archaeology of the Middle East. Rather than admit that they are looking to profit off of the region, they paint a picture of noble intentions for culture. According to a section of their website devoted to the project:

"We as scholars feel that the cultural product we offer has an intense, if somewhat intangible, value – by showing the great significance of the past for our common societal advancement. Our logo signifies just such a relationship: two deities are shown supporting jointly a standard – symbolizing the two worlds of business and academia holding up our shared cultural values."

Unfortunately, due to potential copyright infringement, I cannot include a picture of the actual logo; however I will post it on my blog for all to see. While it is not completely out of the ordinary to read that big oil has shady international dealings, it is not acceptable.

The list of supporters goes on to include PricewaterhouseCoopers, a huge multinational taxation firm headquartered in London. PricewaterhouseCoopers was found to be unethically favored by the World Bank in a bid to privatize the water distribution system in India. This is just another example of how corporate interests threaten cultures and struggle for control over the world's resources.

Also involved in funding this excavation is The British Foreign Commonwealth office that works with 12 agencies and public bodies, including the Government Communications Headquarters, BBC, and Secret Intelligence Service. The list also includes support from SKA International Group, The British Institute for the Study of Iraq, Technical Solutions to Industry FZE, F.H. Al-Salman & Co, IKB Travel, and BSOC.

Then, there is the founding donor, Baron Lorne von Thyssen of the Thyssen family dynasty. Lorne Thyssen, is heir to one of the richest families in the world. It is widely accepted that the Thyssen family owns the world's largest and most valuable private collection of relics and art said to be rivaled only by that of Queen Elizabeth.

So where did the Thyssen family get their massive fortune? Originating from Germany, Thyssen family members have taken up residence in various countries and spread in a corporate imperialist fashion, much like the Rothschild banking family. The Thyssen family has many notable members, all of whom descend from Friedrich Thyssen, who established steel works, elevators, escalators, industrial conglomerates, banks, and massive art collections.

This family is one of the many mega rich bloodline based powerhouses that maintain control over world affairs in secrecy. Their roots go way back and their propensity to fund nefarious causes is apparent as we will see in the case of Fritz Thyssen.

Fritz Thyssen was the first man to get the newly formed Nazi party off the ground by giving them a large injection of funds ($25,000) in the mid-1920's. In 1931, he joined the Nazi Party, and soon became close friends with Adolf Hitler. He continued to use his offshore banks to pump money into the Nazi war machine.

Over the years, Thyssen came to be known as "Hitler's most important and prominent financier". When asked about Hitler, Thyssen was actually quoted as saying, "I realized his orator gifts and his ability to lead the masses. What impressed me most, however, was the order that reigned over his meetings, the almost military discipline of his followers." Thyssen also persuaded the Association of German Industrialists to donate 3 million Reichsmarks to the Nazi Party for the 1933 Reichstag election. As a payback, he was in turn elected a Nazi member of the Reichstag and appointed to the Prussian State Council, the largest German state.

Fritz Thyssen, ca. 1928.

After WWII, Thyssen was tried for being a Nazi supporter, which he did not deny, admitting his support for the exclusion of Jews from German business and mistreatment of his own Jewish employees in the 1930s. One of the banking institutions founded by Thyssen to help funnel money to the Nazi party was the Union Banking Corporation (UBC). UBC was a place where Thyssen strategically installed his friends in positions of power. These were not just any friends. These were members of what he referred to as "The Order".

Upon cross-referencing the names on this list, you will find that the order referred to here is the Skull & Bones. Skull & Bones is an undergraduate senior secret society at Yale University, founded in 1832. It was originally named "the Order of the Skull and Bones". Here is the list of men installed by Thyssen to run his organizations:

1. **E. Roland Harriman** — *(The Order 1917)* Vice President of W.A. Harriman & Co., New York

2. **H.J. Kouwenhoven** — *(Nazi)* Nazi banker, managing partner of August Thyssen Bank and Bankvoor Handel Scheepvaart N.V. (the transfer bank for Thyssen's funds)

3. **Knight Woolley** — *(The Order 1917)* Director of Guaranty Trust, New York, and Director of the Federal Reserve Bank of New York

4. **Cornelius Lievense** — President, Union Banking Corp. and Director of Holland-American Investment Corp.

5. **Ellery Sedgewick James** — *(The Order 1917)* Partner, Brown Brothers, & Co., New York

6. **Johann Groninger** — *(Nazi)* Director of Bank voor Handel en Scheepvaart and Vereinigte Stahlwerke (Thyssen's steel operations)

7. **J.L. Guinter** — Director Union Banking Corp.

8. **Prescott Sheldon Bush** — *(The Order 1917)* Partner, Brown Brothers, Harriman. Father of President G. H. W. Bush

So let's review some points that stick out right away. Four directors of UBC are members of The Order, all initiated at Yale in 1917, meaning, they were members of the same Yale class. All four were members of the same cell (club) D 115. Guaranty Trust, the organization represented by Knight Woolley who later became the director of the Federal Reserve Bank of N.Y.

Where have we seen "Woolley" before? Remember the first "archaeologist" who discovered the massive treasures at Ur, Sir Charles Leonard Woolley, son of George Herbert Woolley? Speaking of George Herbert, it is equally interesting to note that Prescott Sheldon Bush (The Order 1917), father of George Herbert Walker Bush, was the business partner of Nazi financier, Fritz Thyssen.

One thing is clear, out of eight directors of Thyssen's bank in New York, UBC, there are at least six who are confirmed as either

Nazis or members of Skull and Bones. The Nazis were known to be unusually interested in archaeological discoveries and excavations, particularly those that they thought could prove their claims about human origins. The Nazis were obsessed with bloodlines and what they referred to as "racial hygiene". This is a term generously provided to the Nazis by their valued staff of anthropologist/eugenists.

Skull and Crossbones c1947, GHW Bush is left of clock.

I would urge anyone reading this to do the research for themselves. Peek down the rabbit hole and you will find that it goes even deeper than I have been able to describe in this report. All of it is out there as public record, hidden in plain site. The Thyssen family continues to head a mega-wealthy elite empire seeking to control the world's resources, including its cultural resources. This is why even now, ties remain strong between big oil, banking, archaeology, and power. As a major collector of artifacts and art, Baron Lorne von Thyssen remains heavily invested in the project at Tell Khaiber.

Described as a Hollywood style playboy, Baron Lorne von Thyssen, is an interesting character, to say the least. Benefitting from the billionaire success of his family dynasty, he has enjoyed a life of luxury and exclusivity. He moved from London to America as an aspiring actor, hoping to succeed in show business. About his father, Baron 'Heini' Thyssen-Bornemisza, he once boasted "with private jet, yacht, a large staff, seven homes, and well, not quite a footman behind each chair. He lives like a 19th century grand seigneur!" Baron Lorne von Thyssen speaks of dining with the King of Spain at the new home of the Thyssen-Bornemisza collection at the Villahermosa Palace in Madrid. Germany, Britain, France, and the United States all vied to house the £800 million collection of some of the world's most treasured works of art.

Lamenting that his childhood was "a gilded cage", he was raised by a nanny and was left entirely to her care while his sister was sent abroad to various schools. Baron Lorne von Thyssen has also described his mother as a mere "ghostly apparition one saw during meal times". As for his father, he didn't have a lot of contact with

him either, seeing him only as a "hugely powerful, daunting figure."
When Baron Lorne von Thyssen was 17, he was expelled for getting drunk and throwing up on the headmaster's feet. After years of alcoholism and undergoing extensive psychiatric treatment, he converted to Islam and continues to collect ancient art.

So why does any of this matter? So what if wealthy people who have an interest in ancient art fund excavations in war torn countries. Would we really want government doing it instead?

These are some of the questions some may consider when looking at this information. Here is something else to consider. On the roster of supporters I had listed earlier, included was The British Foreign Commonwealth office that works with 12 agencies and public bodies, including the Government Communications Headquarters, BBC, and Secret Intelligence Service. Part of their priorities, as stated on their official website include, foreign affairs and climate change. Interestingly, the team is sent to investigate part of what is referred to an "environmental archaeology team" from the British government's Environmental Archaeology Unit. This is a sort of archaeological green police, so to speak. The mission for their research is to find evidence of climate change. The researchers have stated that they are not interested in focusing on relics and artifacts, just climate change. I find it difficult to believe that it is that cut and dry.

So here we have a complex issue of varying agendas funding a project with major implications for humanity. Continuing my investigation into the latest discover near Ur, I have found even more unusual ties that I will publish in another report, just as soon as I am finished. I have also found more sources and more leads into what has actually been discovered. So where do we go from here?

FIVE

Moving Forward

. . . . . .

POTTERY AND ARTIFACTS SITTING ON THE SURFACE have been systematically collected, bagged up, and shipped out for further analysis. Fragments of vessels made from stone including a piece of ivory have also been excavated. Various tools made of copper and stone, a rim fragment from a once magnificent alabaster bowl, and not one, but two molded clay plaques showing a male worshipper and a female figure, respectively

It gets even more interesting. A mysterious item made from rare and expensive diorite has been found and has baffled archaeologists. Diorite is a gray rock that is relatively rare and extremely hard, making it notoriously difficult to work with. It is so hard that ancient civilizations used diorite balls to work granite. The use of diorite in art was important in Mesopotamian empires and was even used by both the Inca and Mayan civilizations for fortress walls and weaponry. Theories for what this artifact is have been a recycled chip from larger relic or possibly a game piece. No one knows for sure.

Also found was the shallow grave of an infant, just under the surface. It is unclear what the gender of the infant is, but its body had been placed into a pottery jar which was then laid on its side.

Finally, the answer to the question that had been on *my* mind. Found at the site were three tablet fragments, right on the surface. This is astonishing since they are made of unbaked clay, leading them to be very fragile. The tablet fragments have been sent for analysis but there are clues as to what they said. One is a partial lists men's names, along with their father's names, which indicates a record of elite bloodlines and patriarchal lineage. They are all Babylonian in origin. Another tablet fragment says there is the 'something' (a piece was missing here) of the Governor that was in the city. So the settlement at Tell Khaiber was apparently important enough to have a governor. The administrative center theory is really taking hold. Another tablet piece makes mention of orchards and gardens, like those in the Garden of Eden.

I have been asked by a number of people about the potential of locating a specific lost technology. A structure with great power, often referred to as a stargate. Since I am unable to go to the site in Iraq and see such a structure with my own eyes, I believe it would be irresponsible for me to speculate on such a topic. However, I will say this; a gradiometer was brought in and used to measure the site's magnetic field.

Although it is not highly unusual that a site like this would be surveyed with a magnetometer, it is still notable. A gradiometer is a special type of magnetometer with multiple sensors: one closer to the ground to collect magnetic data about the surface, and the other located above the first sensor to collect information about the Earth's magnetic field. The archaeologist would then subtract one reading from the other, essentially filtering out the noise from the Earth's magnetic field, allowing subtle features of archaeological interest to be detected.

Therefore, the explanation for this is that the gradiometer would record magnetic differences between the walls and rooms without disturbing the deposits underneath so they could better locate any buildings. This is logical, but it is still interesting to consider that this site's magnetic field is actively being researched. So I'll leave that for others to think of what they will.

As I mentioned, I will keep on this to provide the public with all that I can on this amazing and important discovery.

So again, why should we care what big oil, mining, and energy corporations, global taxation firms, aristocratic families, and a host of other nefarious groups do in the desert in another country? Let the egg-heads dig for dusty little pottery shards at the expense of the wealthy. Right?

Wrong! This is the apathetic and cynical stance the establishment wants us to take. That way, they can rob the world of cultural heritage and keep humanity in the dark at the expense of struggling war torn communities. They want to hypnotize us with panem et circenses, or the bread and circuses of modernity. If we are sitting slack-jawed in front of a television, poisoned by the edible food like substances of the industrial food chain, and ignorant to our own power, nothing will ever change for the better.

I felt that sense of powerlessness upon first learning of the discovery. I read the plea of someone living in a distant land, as I sat comfortably in my pajamas and office chair, staring at a screen and thought, "What can I do? I have no power.". If those thoughts creep in, as they have been programmed to do, do your very best to fight it. Tell yourself that you do have the power to make a difference. Galileo Galilei said, "All truths are easy to understand once they are discovered; the point is to discover them." Discovery is a necessary part of understanding the truth.

Archaeology is an area where people can join in getting excited about learning who we are and why we are here. Discoveries made can become a source of national pride and unity through the recognition of a shared heritage. Archaeology has the power to bring people together. This powerful connection people have to their cultural resources has been seen as a threat throughout history and it is no different today. If you systematically erase the past, you can control the future.

Stripping a nation of its cultural material robs it of identity. Without cultural identity, social cohesion gradually dissolves, and people are more easily homogenized and controlled. Not only is it important for human identity, discoveries in economically challenged areas can benefit from their cultural resources by creating employment in museums, universities, archives, security, and the sites as well as through exhibitions that attract tourists. It can be an economic boom.

Some hard facts, according to UNESCO:

1. The African continent has been the subject of intense looting since pre-colonial times and this has continued unabated throughout the colonial and post-colonial eras.

2. Africa, as well as Southeast Asia, China, Latin America and the Middle East, is a major source market for the illicit trade due to the abundance in heritage treasures.

3. The existence of lucrative markets in the West ensure that the artifacts end up in its museums and private collections.

4. Estimates on African cultural material currently out of Africa range from 50-90%.

5. Recent articles indicate that there are more Dogon in France than in Mali.

You are not allowed to buy such rare artifacts, so why should billionaire art hoarding families be able to, so long as they launder their money through grants to archaeology departments? All around the world, millions of people are beginning to wake up to the truth about who we are and where we come from. Through the sharing of ideas and theories, while keeping an open-mind and a compassionate heart, we can start to realize the change we all yearn for. Though many people in the truth movement may have varying ideologies or causes dear to them, one thing I am sure we can all agree on is the importance of freedom.

We must fight for freedom of individuality through unity. We must embrace our heritage, learn from our differences, and stop using pejorative labels such as "fringe" or "pseudo" , as these are divisive, and counterproductive to the true scientific method. Let us strive to be non-conformists working in unison for the common good. "Conformity is the jailer of freedom and the enemy of growth." (John Fitzgerald Kennedy). Let's turn off the television, roll up our sleeves and explore our past together so that we all recognize our true potentials regardless of credentials, net worth, belief systems, or any other factor that could limit our success. Just as there are no limits to our universal consciousness, there are no limits at all for a truly free society.

SIX

More Information

. . . . . .

About the author: Heather Lynn is a writer, researcher, and archaeologist with a PhD in comparative religion. She is president of the Society for Truth in Archaeological Research and a member of the World Archaeological Congress. Her research topics include hidden history, mythology, metaphysics and the origin of consciousness. She lives near Cleveland, Ohio. To contact Dr. Heather Lynn, you may email her at heather@drheather-lynn.com. You can also find her on Facebook.